Book 1
Facebook Social Power
BY SAM KEY

&

Book 2
HTML Professional Programming Made Easy

BY SAM KEY

Book 1
Facebook Social Power

BY SAM KEY

The Most Powerful Represented Facebook Guide to Making Money on anything on the Planet!

Programming Box Set #89: Facebook Social Power & HTML Professional Programming Made Easy

Table Of Contents

Introduction

I want to thank you and congratulate you for purchasing the book, “Learning the Social Power of Facebook: The Most Powerful Represented Facebook Guide to Making Money on anything on the Planet!”

This book contains proven steps and strategies on how to learn ways to use Facebook as a means to generate money for whatever business you have.

As you well may know by now, Facebook can be an amazing tool to promote your business, and of course, make money from it. However, not everyone knows how to do it, but with the help of this book, you’ll learn everything you need to know about how to use Facebook to attract people’s attention, and be successful in the world of business.

What are you waiting for? Start reading this book now and make money through Facebook as soon as possible!

Thanks again for purchasing this book, I hope you enjoy it!

Chapter 1: Make Use of Advertising based on E-Commerce

Because of Facebook's Ad Platform, a lot of marketers have been able to reach a wide range of audience because they get to put ads on their Facebook Pages that takes those who click the links to E-Commerce sites, so just the fact that these people get to see their pages already add a lot of traffic to their sites, and may allow people to get paid.

Oftentimes, people overlook the ads-to-direct sites but knowing how to go forth with it is very beneficial because it has a three-way approach that will help you earn a lot of money. Basically, this approach goes as follows:

FB Ads—Discount Pages/Website Sales—Buyers/Customers

One example of a company that benefited a lot from E-Commerce based Advertising through Facebook is Vamplets.com. Vamplets.com is popular for selling plush dolls—but these dolls aren't just regular plush dolls, as they are Vampire Plushies. When Vamplets used this kind of advertising, they were able to achieve 300% ROI, which is definitely a mean feat.

So, how then are you going to be able to use E-Commerce based Advertising for your business? Follow the pointers below and you'll understand how.

Choose your Audience

First and foremost, you have to choose your target demographic so that sales funnel will be easier to be filled. Facebook will allow you to choose between one of the following:

- Custom Audience from Your Website
- Custom Audience from MailChimp
- Data File Custom Audience
- Custom Audience from Your Mobile App

Once you're able to choose your target demographic, it will be easy for you to convert an ad to money because these people will be interested in what you have to offer because you're no longer going to be generalizing things.

You can also choose your audience via the Facebook Audience Insights Category. Here, you'll be able to find people who are interested in your campaign, based on pages that they have liked, so that you'd know that they would like to see what your business is all about. This is called interest-based campaigning.

You can also try using Lookalike Audiences. You can do this by making use of your existing audience, and then pick the next group of people who act and feel similar to your original audience so your posts would be able to reach more people, and you'd get more traffic and revenue, as well. It would be nice to test audiences, too, so you'd know who's interested in your services.

For example, you're selling clothes for pregnant women. You really cannot expect people who are single or who are still in High School click your ads, or like your page, because of course, they're not in that stage of their lives yet. So, make sure that you choose audiences that you know will listen to what you have to say.

Then, go on and place a Facebook Pixel to the footer of your page, and your ads will then be connected to Facebook. You can also choose to send traffic to one audience group this week, then to another group the next.

Make Proper Segments for Visitors of Your Homepage

Of course, you have to make sure that your homepage gets the attention of many because if it doesn't, and if people feel alienated by it, you also cannot expect that you'll gain profit from it. The three basic things that you have to have in your homepage include:

- New Sales Items
- Branding Ads
- Other Promotional Ads

Make Segments for Categories and Products

You can also place ads in various categories of your website so that even if your customer does not check out all the items he placed in the cart, your website will still gain some revenue because more often than not, customers like to buy products based on ads that were able to get through to them.

Chapter 2: Use Fan Marketing E-Commerce

Basically, Fan Marketing E-Commerce is the means of promoting your business by making sure that you post ads through your page and have those ads appear on the newsfeeds of your target demographic.

Research has it that fans become more interested in a new product or business when they see ads, instead of when they learn about the said products through contests or just from other people. Why? Simply because ads are more professional ways of getting people's attention and marketing products, and Facebook definitely makes that easy.

However, it's not enough that you just have a fanpage. You have to make sure that you actually use the said page and that it doesn't get stuck. You can do this by making sure that you constantly post a thing or two, and that you interact with your fans, as well.

You see, a study held in 2011 showed that although over a hundred thousand people may like a certain page, sometimes, revenue only gets up by 7%, because the owners of the fan pages do not interact with their fans and have not posted anything in a while. You also have to make sure that you stay relevant by being able to attract new fans from time to time.

Once you do this right, you'll be able to create the process of:

FB Ads—FB Fans—See Posts—Click to Website—Buyers/Customers

Some of those who have greatly benefited from Fan Marketing Strategies include:

- Baseball Roses, a company that sells artificial roses made from old baseball balls, who gained over 437% of ROI with the help of Facebook Fan Marketing;
- Superherostuff.com, a website that sells merchandise based on famous superheroes, such as t-shirts, jackets, hoodies, shoes, and more, gained over 150% ROI, and;

- Rosehall Kennel Breeds, a company that specializes in selling German Shepherds, gained over a whopping 4,000% of ROI for its fan acquisition speed alone—and that's definitely something that should inspire you.

So, what exactly did these companies do and how did they make use of Facebook Fan Marketing E-Commerce for their own benefit? Here are some tips that you can follow:

1. **Make sure that you post a new update after your last update is gone from people's newsfeeds.** Sometimes, you see posts in your feed for even a day or two after posting, but there are also times when they are gone after just a couple of minutes or hours. It actually varies due to how fans see or react on those posts and Facebook's EdgeRank Algorithm will be able to give you a glimpse of how your post is doing, based on three main factors, which are:

    a. **Likes per Post.** You'd know that people are interested in your posts when they actually make it a point to like the said posts, and it's great because likes are always updated in real time, and will also let your posts stay longer on people's newsfeeds. Therefore, make sure to check the numbers of likes regularly.

    b. **Comments per Post.** Comments are always time-stamped, but you cannot always rely on these as not everyone like to comment on posts, and you cannot define whether the posts appear on people's feeds, or they're simply too lazy to comment.

    c. **Impressions per Post.** This is basically the number of times a single status has been viewed. While the numbers update as more and more people get to see your post, there are also times when the number stay stagnant only because Facebook refuses to update, so may have to wait a while to see the real numbers.

A good way of trying to gauge your influence on Facebook is by posting an hourly status, then make sure that you record the number of likes, comments, and impressions, and then record the data on Excel. Make a graph, then see the ratio of how much your posts appear on one's feeds, and decide the average number of posts that you have to do per day or per week.

2. **Make sure that the things you post are not redundant.** People these days have really short attention span so it would be nice if you know how to post varied content. Make sure that your fans have something to come back to each day, and that they don't get bored with whatever it is that you have on your website and won't click the "dislike" button.
3. **Do some marketing.** Again, you're trying to make money by means of promoting your products so you have to do a lot of marketing via Facebook. An easy way of doing this is by giving your fans discount codes that they can use if they're interested in buying your products so that they'd constantly check your page.
4. **Make sure that social sharing buttons are open.** While you may use Facebook as the original platform for advertising your services, you also have to realize that it's important to share your content on other websites or social networking sites so that more people would get to see what you have to offer. Also, make sure that your page is set to public because you really cannot expect people to know what you want them to know if your page is set to private. When your page is public, they'll be able to like, comment, and share your posts, which will bring you more traffic and more revenue. Then, connect your Facebook Page to your other social media accounts so that whenever you post updates on your Facebook Page, the updates will be sent to all your other accounts, as well.
5. **Don't ever try hard-selling tactics.** It's always better to be subtle because people hate it when they feel like their feeds are full of pages that just sell their products outright without making the fans understand what they're all about. So, try asking your fans some questions, or create polls about what kind of products or services they like but never just put up ads or ask them to "buy your products" right away without helping them know that you're their "friend" and that you want them to know what's best in the market right now. You can also place behind the scenes videos of what goes on in your company, or

post testimonials from past customers to get the curiosity of your fans running. This way, you get to be trustworthy and your business will be more authoritative, and people would be more interested.

6. **And, make sure that you provide good customer service.** For a Facebook Page to be successful, it doesn't have to be bombarded with ads, you also have to make sure that you get to be friends with your customers and that loyalty and trust are built. For example, when one of your fans posts questions or queries on your page, take time to answer the said questions, and make sure that you reply as soon as possible so that you get to create some sense of urgency and that people will know that you're there.

Keep these tips in mind and you'll surely be able to make use of your Facebook Page to give you a lot of profit. Oh, and make sure to have ample amounts of patience, too!

Chapter 3: Connect Facebook Ads to E-Mail

Another way of making use of Facebook to gain revenue is by connecting ads to e-mails. Basically, it's a way of promoting content to your e-mail subscribers so that it will be easier for your fans to know about your new products or services, or to know if there are contests or events coming up based on the updates that you have sent.

Basically, when Facebook ads are sent to people's e-mails, there are more chances of acquiring a larger number of future subscribers. And Facebook makes this easy for you as they have a feature that allows you to add E-mail lists to your Fan Page so that whenever you post an update, your e-mail list will automatically get to know it, too.

The target formula is as follows:

FB Ad—Squeeze—E-mail Sign Up—E-mail Open—E-mail Click to Visit—Buyers/Customers

So, in order for you to be successful in this kind of marketing tactic, you first have to get a target demographic of e-mail subscribers. While it may be easy to just post an invite so your fans would want to be part of your e-mail list, it will be nice to filter people who probably won't open your e-mails and choose people who would be interested in what you have to offer. You can do this by adding information to the Facebook Ad Copy Page. The information that you need are as follows:

- Gender
- Age
- Location
- Interests
- Relationship Status
- Educational Attainment/Level
- Workplace
- Pages that have been liked (So you'd get to see if they would like the posts that you'd be making)

Then, go on and upload the e-mail list on your Facebook Page by giving Facebook a list of e-mails from MailChimp or any other AutoResponder Service, so that the e-mail addresses of your fans will be synchronized to your page.

Effective Message Integration

It's so easy to send a message but it's never really easy to make sure that those messages are effective. However, there are a couple of tips that you can keep in mind:

- Optimize Facebook Ad Headlines with Catchy Subject Lines so that your fans will be interested to open your e-mails. Examples include:
    - Do Gamers dream of DOTA II?
    - Why your 12 year old likes Miley Cyrus
    - 8 Most Annoying Social Media Moments of 2014
    - 3 Ways to Improve Your Life

  Basically, you have to make sure that your subject lines have a lot to do with your content and with your line of business so that your fans won't be confused and they'd be interested in what you have to say.

- Add your fans' testimonials and comments about your services so others would know that you are for real.
- Add images into your e-mails. After all, people have short attention span and they would appreciate it if they get to see images as part of your e-mails because these would get their attention more and would help them picture what you are talking about.
- Let your fans know that you are going to send another e-mail blast by updating your Facebook status.
- Tease some of the contents of your e-mail on your status updates so that your fans will be hyped up and will be curious to open their e-mails.

- Make use of Facebook Landing Tabs, and Social Log-in Software, so that whenever your fans open their e-mails, it will automatically add traffic to your Facebook Page, and your website, as well.
- Put some sort of disclaimer, or a line that allows your fans to unsubscribe if they want to, because they have to know that you're not actually forcing them to read your messages and that they have the choice to unsubscribe from your list.
- And don't forget to send Thank You messages. If you want to foster a great relationship with your fans, you have to let them know that you're thankful that they're around, and that they're part of your list, so that they will realize that it's substantial to read the content that you are sending, and that it's important to be a fan of yours, instead of just talking about yourself all the time, without thinking of your fans. After all, without them, you won't gain any profit so you have to be grateful that they're around.

You can also run Geo-targeted ads, or ads that are meant for people who live in one location alone, so that the e-mails would feel more personal and so that your fans will know that you are really thinking of them. Sometimes, targeting people who are in the same vicinity as you is more effective because you get to really connect with them as you experience the same things and you'd know that they are more likely to try your products, unlike those that live in far away places.

If you're able to be successful with Facebook E-mail marketing, you can definitely gain more traffic and more revenue. One of those Fortune 500 Companies actually gained 400% ROI just because of its e-mail subscribers, so you can expect that you'll gain more, too, but only if you follow the tips given above. Good Luck!

Chapter 4: Making Use of Your Ad-Supported Sites

Ad-Supported sites are those that run advertisements and allow the said ads to be shared to your Facebook Page.

This is especially helpful for those whose businesses are really situated online, and those whose blogs or websites are their bread and butter. So, if that's the case, it would be important to create a Facebook Page that's connected to your blog or your website so that things would be formalized more. People like it when they see that a certain website has a Facebook Page because they feel like they'd get to be updated more without having to go to the website.

The formula for this is as follows:

FB Ad—FB Fan—See Post—Click to Website—Click Ad

So basically, when people click ads on your website that take them to your Facebook Page and Vice Versa, you not only gain traffic, you get to be paid, as well. This is similar as the popular Pay-Per-Click Advertising tactic. And also, when you get more fans from various parts of the world, your revenue will increase even more mainly because your content now gets to reach a large number of people, which evidently is beneficial for your business.

Proud Single Moms, a site targeted to help single mothers, gained over $5,000 for Facebook Ads alone that were promoted on their Facebook Page that has around 100,000 fans. On their blog, they made sure that they posted topics that single mothers would be able to relate to, and they also made sure that they used keywords that would give them high search rank on search engines such as Google, or Yahoo.

You can make use of Keyword Tools that are found online to find the perfect keywords that are related to your niche. Once you use these keywords in your posts, you'll be able to generate traffic and revenue.

The main reason why ads on Facebook are so effective is the fact that almost everyone in the world has a Facebook account, so of course, you can expect them to see your posts and the ads that are on your page, too. Plus, when you post links of your blog's content to your Facebook Page, there are more chances that people will get to read these posts because of course, they found it on Facebook, and they didn't use the web just so they could see your website. And these days, that is very important. The key is to be reachable.

Proud Single Moms made sure that they posted the links of blog post updates each day and in just a matter of six months, they were able to create another website that gave them more revenue.

Chapter 5: Other Tips

Aside from the techniques given above, you can also make use of these Facebook Marketing tactics to make sure that your business gains more profit:

Ads through SMS

While it may not be as popular as other Facebook Marketing tips, the combination of Facebook Ads and Text Messaging have slowly been gaining the attention of many for being a fast-paced approach when it comes to advertising products and services. In fact, around 24% of marketers on mobile have gained more ROI just because people have responded to text messages regarding product promotions, and have tried the coupons that they gave away through text, too.

This is especially effective for those with business that are related to food as free coupons that were sent to Facebook fans helped these fans to be more interested to try certain products that were being sold, and have visited the restaurants more often in hopes that they'd be given more information and more freebies, too. When people feel like they know the latest news about a certain establishment or a certain product, it's easy for them to appreciate the said establishment and so they get to patronize it more. This then gave the restaurants around $60,000 more revenue, which is definitely something good!

Give Some Offers that they won't be able to refuse!

Mostly everyone want freebies, because money is really hard to come by these days and not everything is affordable, so of course, they feel like it's nice to be able to get some goodies or services for free. Facebook Offers actually help you create deals with your fans that are not available on other social media platforms.

Basically, you ask your customers to like your page and leave their e-mail addresses so that you can send them coupons or offers that they can redeem in your store. First, make the offers exclusive to your fans then when it gets successful, you can then make more offers for people outside your circle so that more people would be excited to try your products and see what you have to offer.

Don't think about losing profit. More often than not, when you give things away for free, people will be more interested to try your other products and so of course, they'd be paying you in the future, so it's like you have made them your investment and soon enough, you'll benefit from them.

Create Apps for them

A lot of people these days rely on apps that they could use to open certain websites or pages, and of course, if you create an app for your business, it will be easy for them to read your content and it will be easy for you to reach them. They wouldn't have to deal with the hassle of using the browser just so they could see some offers or read articles connected to a certain topic that they would like to learn about. Also, it's better if you add links to your Facebook Page to the app that you have created so that everything will be merged together.

You can also create Facebook Ads without creating a Facebook Page

You can do this by selecting the Clicks to Website option of Facebook or the Website Conversions tab. People will still get to see your ads on the right side of their pages. You know, those ads that appear near the chat sidebar, so in a way, you still get to promote your business, but having Facebook Pages are still way better because then the ads appear on the main feeds and not just on the right side tabs.

Create a catchy headline

Just like how important it is to create effective e-mail subject lines, it's also important to create catchy ad headlines because these will attract people's attention and will allow people to understand what you and your business are all about.

The rule of thumb is to make sure that the headline of your ad is the same as the title of your page so it will be easily recognizable. It would also be helpful if you pair it up with an image that you have created so that people will be able to connect the said image to your business and it will be easy for them to remember your ad.

Make use of Sponsored Stories, too

You see, sponsored stories are the results of how people interact on your page or how they appreciate your content. Basically, whenever someone likes your posts or updates, or when they comment on or share your content, it creates "Facebook Stories". To make sure that these stories appear on a lot of people's newsfeeds, you have to pay a minimal fee, so it's like you get to easily advertise your content and you make sure that people actually get to see them.

But make sure that you choose the best bidding and advertising options

What's good about Facebook is that it allows you to choose the best kind of bidding option that will be good for your business. For example, you can choose whether you want to gain revenue through clicks, or through impressions then you can then reach your objective after you have customized your bids.

You can also choose whether you'd like to pay for your content to be advertised by paying daily, or by paying for a lifetime. The advantages of paying for a lifetime is that you'd know that your content will always be published and that you'd basically have nothing else to worry about, but the thing is that when you want to change the products you are advertising or if you're going to close your business down, it's like you'll get people confused because they'll still see ads from your old site, and they'd keep looking for your services. So, it's recommended that you just pay for the ads daily or on a case to case basis, say there's an event that's coming up and the like, so that it won't be hard for you to reach your followers and gain potential fans in the process, too.

When making use of image ads, make sure that text is only 20%

You would not want to bombard your followers with too many texts and images in just one post. Plus, your image ads won't be approved if they contain more than 20% of text.

In order to know if your ads are following Facebook's guidelines, check out the Facebook Grid Tool that will help you see how your ad looks and what needs to be changed, if necessary.

Let others help you

Sometimes, two heads are better than one, and it's great because when you add another admin to your page, they can also update your page so whenever you're busy or if you cannot answer queries right away, these other admins can help you out.

Just make sure that you choose admins that you can trust and that they know a lot about your business so the things they will be posting will be substantial, too. To do this, just go to the Ad Manager option of Facebook, then click Ad Account Roles, and choose Add a User. Make sure that the person you will add as an admin is your friend on Facebook and that his e-mail address can easily be searched through Facebook, too.

And, don't forget to choose the revenue model that is right for you

To do this, you may have to try each technique first, but don't worry because sooner or later, you'll find the one that proves to be the most effective for your business.

In the marketing business, trial and error really is one of the biggest keys to success, so don't worry if you feel like you aren't being successful right away. Take chances and soon enough, you'll be on the path to success. Good Luck!

Conclusion

Thank you again for purchasing this book!

I hope this book was able to help you understand how you can use Facebook to advertise your business and gain lots of revenue.

The next step is to follow the techniques listed here, and don't be afraid to try each one because sooner or later, you'll find the perfect fit for you. Advertise through Facebook and let your business soar!

Thank you and good luck!

Book 2
HTML Professional Programming Made Easy

BY SAM KEY

Expert HTML Programming Language Success in a Day for any Computer Users

Programming Box Set #89: Facebook Social Power & HTML Professional Programming Made Easy

Table Of Contents

Introduction

I want to thank you and congratulate you for purchasing the book, *Professional HTML Programming Made Easy: Expert HTML Programming Language Success In A Day for any Computer User!*

This book contains proven steps and strategies on how to create a web page in just a day. And if you have a lot of time in a day, you will be able to create a decent and informative website in two or three days.

HTML programming or development lessons are sometimes used as an introductory resource to programming and is a prerequisite to learning web development. In this book, you will be taught of the fundamentals of HTML. Mastering the contents of this book will make web development easier for you and will allow you to grasp some of the basics of computer programming.

To get ready for this book, you will need a desktop or laptop. That is all. You do not need to buy any expensive HTML or website development programs. And you do not need to rent a server or subscribe to a web hosting service. If you have questions about those statements, the answers are in the book.

Thanks again for purchasing this book. I hope you enjoy it!

Chapter 1: Getting Started with HTML

This book will assume that you have no prior knowledge on HTML. Do not skip reading any chapters or this book if you plan to learn about CSS, JavaScript, or any other languages that is related to web development.

HTML is a markup language. HTML defines what will be displayed on your browser and how it will be displayed. To program or code HTML, all you need is a text editor. If your computer is running on a Windows operating system, you can use Notepad to create or edit HTML files. Alternatively, if your computer is a Mac, you can use TextEdit instead.

Why is this book telling you to use basic text editors? Why are expert web developers using HTML creation programs such as Adobe Dreamweaver to create their pages? Those programs are supposed to make HTML coding easier, right?

You do not need them yet. Using one will only confuse you, especially if you do not know the fundamentals of HTML. Aside from that, web designing programs such as Adobe Dreamweaver are not all about dragging and dropping items on a web page. You will also need to be capable of manually writing the HTML code that you want on your page. That is why those programs have different views like Design and Code views. And most of them time, advanced developers stay and work more using the Code view, which is similar to a typical text editing program.

During your time learning HTML using this book, create a folder named HTML on your desktop. As you progress, you will see snippets of HTML code written here. You can try them out using your text editor and browser. You can save them as HTML files, place them into the HTML folder, and open them on your browser to see what those snippets of codes will do.

Your First HTML Page

Open your text editor and type the following in it:

Hello World!
After writing that line on your text editor, save it. On the save file dialog box, change the name of the file as firstexample.html. Do not forget the .html part. That part will serve as your file's file extension. It denotes that the file that you have saved is an HTML file and can be opened by the web browsers you have in your computer. Make sure that your program was able to save it as an .html file. Some text editor programs might still automatically add another file extension on your file name, so if that happens, you will not be open that file in your browser normally.

By the way, you do not need to upload your HTML file on a website or on the internet to view it. As long as your computer can access it, you can open it. And since your first HTML page will be in your computer, you can open it with your browser. After all, a web site can be viewed as a folder on the internet that contains HTML files that you can open.

When saving the file, make sure that it is being saved as plain text and not rich or formatted text. By default, programs such as Microsoft Word or WordPad save text files as formatted. If you saved the file as formatted, your browser might display the HTML code you have written incorrectly.

To open that file, you can try one of the three common ways. The first method is to double click or open the file normally. If you were able to save the file with the correct file extension, your computer will automatically open a browser to access the file.

The second method is to use the context menu (if you are using Windows). Right click on the file, and hover on the open with option. The menu will expand, and the list of programs that can open an HTML file will be displayed to you. Click on the browser that you want to use to open the file.

The third method is to open your browser. After that, type the local file address of your file. If you are using Windows 7 and you saved the file on the HTML folder in your desktop, then you can just type in C:\Users\User\Desktop\HTML\firstexample.html. The folder User may change depending on the account name you are using on your computer to login.

Once you have opened the file, it will show you the text you have written on it. Congratulations, you have already created a web page. You can just type paragraphs of text in the file, and it will be displayed by your browsers without problem. It is not the fanciest method, but it is the start of your journey to learn HTML.

You might be wondering, is it that easy? To be honest, yes. Were you expecting complex codes? Well, that will be tackled on the next chapter. And just to give you a heads up, it will not be complex.

This chapter has just given you an idea what is an HTML file and how you create, edit, and open one in your computer. The next chapter will discuss about tags, attributes, and elements.

Chapter 2: Elements, Properties, Tags, and Attributes

Of course, you might be already thinking: "Web pages do not contain text only, right?" Yes, you are right. In this part of the book, you will have a basic idea about how HTML code works, and how you can place some links on your page.

A web page is composed of elements. A picture on a website's gallery is an element. A paragraph on a website's article is also an element. A hyperlink that directs to another page is an element, too. But how can you do that with text alone? If you can create a web page by just using a text editor, how can you insert images on it?

Using Tags

Well, you can do that by using tags and attributes. By placing tags on the start and end of a text, you will be able to indicate what element it is. It might sound confusing, so below is an example for you to visualize and understand it better and faster:

<p>This is a paragraph that is enclosed on a paragraph tag. This is another sentence. And another sentence.</p>
In the example, the paragraph is enclosed with <p> and </p>. Those two are called HTML tags. If you enclose a block of text inside those two, the browser will understand that the block of text is a paragraph element.

Before you go in further about other HTML tags, take note that there is syntax to follow when enclosing text inside HTML tags. First, an HTML tag has two parts. The first part is the opening or starting tag. And the second part is the closing or ending tag.

The opening tag is enclosed on angled brackets or chevrons (the ones that you use to denote inequality – less and greater than signs). The closing tag, on the other hand, is also enclosed on angled brackets, but it includes a forward slash before the tag itself. The forward slash denotes that the tag is an ending tag.

Those two tags must come in pairs when you use them. However, there are HTML tags that do not require them. And they are called null or void tags. This will be discussed in another lesson. For now, stick on learning the usual HTML tags which require both opening and closing tags.

Attributes

When it comes to inserting images and links in your HTML file, you will need to use attributes. Elements have properties. The properties of each element may vary. For example, paragraph elements do not have the HREF property that anchor elements have (the HREF property and anchor element will be discussed shortly).

To change or edit those properties, you need to assign values using attributes tags. Remember, to indicate an element, use tags; to change values of the properties of elements, use attributes. However, the meanings and relations of those terms might change once you get past HTML and start learning doing CSS and JavaScript. Nevertheless, hold on to that basic idea first until you get further in web development.

Anyway, you will not actually use attributes, but you will need to indicate or assign values on them. Below is an example on how to insert a link on your web page that you will require you to assign a value on an attribute:

```
<a href=”www.google.com” >Google</a>
```

If ever you copied that, pasted or written it on your HTML file, and open your file on a browser, you will see this:

Google

In the example above, the anchor or <a> HTML tag is used. Use the anchor tag when you want to embed a hyperlink or link in your page. Any text between the opening and closing tags of the anchor tag will become the text that will appear as the hyperlink. In the example, it is the word Google that is place between the tags and has appeared on the browser as the link.

You might have noticed the href="www.google.com" part. That part of the line determines on what page your link will direct to when you click it. That part is an example of attribute value assignment. HREF or hypertext reference is an attribute of the anchor tag.

By default, the anchor tag's value is "" or blank. In case that you do not assign any value to that attribute when you use the anchor tag, the anchor element will not become a hyperlink. Try copying and saving this line on your HTML file.

<a>Google</a>
When you open or refresh your HTML file, it will only show the word Google. It will not be underlined or will have a font color of blue. It will be just a regular text. If you hover on it, your mouse pointer will not change into the hand icon; if you click it, your browser will not do anything because the HREF value is blank.

By the way, when you assign a value on an element's or tag's attribute, you must follow proper syntax. The attribute value assignment must be inside the opening tag's chevrons and must be after the text inside the tag.

The attribute assignment must be separated from the tag with a space or spaces. The attribute's name must be type first. It must be followed by an equals sign. Then the value you want to assign to the attribute must follow the equals sign, and must be enclosed with double quotes or single quotes.

Take note, even if the number of spaces between the opening tag and the attribute assignment does not matter much, it is best that you only use one spaces for the sake of readability.

Also, you can place a space between the attribute name and the equals sign or a space between the equals sign and the value that you want to assign to the attribute. However, it is best to adhere to standard practice by not placing a space between them.

When it comes to the value that you want to assign, you can either enclosed them in double or single quotes, but you should never enclose them on a single quote and a double quote or vice versa. If you start with a single quote, end with a single quote, too. Using different quotes will bring problems to your code that will affect the way your browser will display your HTML file.

Nesting HTML Tags

What if you want to insert a link inside your paragraph? How can you do that? Well, in HTML, you can place or nest tags inside tags. Below is an example:

```
<p>This is a paragraph. If you want to go to Google, click this <a
href="www.google.com" >link</a>.</p>
```

If you save that on your HTML file and open your file in your browser, it will appear like this:

This is a paragraph. If you want to go to Google, click this link.

When coding HTML, you will be nesting a lot of elements. Always remember that when nesting tags, never forget the location of the start and closing tags. Make sure that you always close the tags you insert inside a tag before closing the tag you are placing a tag inside on. If you get them mixed up, problems in your page's display will occur. Those tips might sound confusing, so below is an example of a mixed up tag:

```
<p>This is a paragraph. If you want to go to Google, click this <a
href="www.google.com" >link</p>. And this is an example of tags
getting mixed up and closed improperly.</a>
```

In the example, the closing tag for the paragraph tag came first before the closing tag of the anchor tag. If you copied, saved, and opened that, this is what you will get:

This is a paragraph. If you want to go to Google, click this link

. And this is an example of tag that was mixed up and closed improperly.

Since paragraphs are block elements (elements that will be always displayed on the next line and any element after them will be displayed on the next line), the last sentence was shifted to the next line. That is because the code has terminated the paragraph tag immediately.

Also, the anchor tag was closed on the end of the paragraph. Because of that, the word link up to the last word of the last sentence became a hyperlink. You should prevent that kind of mistakes, especially if you are going to code a huge HTML file and are using other complex tags that require a lot of nesting such as table tags. In addition, always be wary of the number of starting and ending tags you use. Missing tags or excess tags can also ruin your web page and fixing and looking for them is a pain.

This chapter has taught you the basic ideas about elements, properties, tags, and attributes. In coding HTML, you will be mostly fiddling around with them. In the next chapter, you will learn how to code a proper HTML document.

Chapter 3: The Standard Structure of HTML

As of now, all you can do are single lines on your HTML file. Though, you might have already tried making a page full of paragraphs and links – thanks to your new found knowledge about HTML tags and attributes. And you might be already hungry to learn more tags that you can use and attributes that you can assign values with.

However, before you tackle those tags and attributes, you should learn about the basic structure of an HTML document. The HTML file you have created is not following the standards of HTML. Even though it does work on your browser, it is not proper to just place random HTML tags on your web page on random places.

In this chapter, you will learn about the html, head, and body tags. And below is the standard structure of an HTML page where those three tags are used:

```
<!DOCTYPE html>
<html>
<head></head>
<body></body>
</html>
```

The Body and the Head

You can split an HTML document in two. The first part is composed of the things that the browser displays on your screen. And the second part is composed of the things that you will not see but is important to your document.

Call the first part as your HTML page's body. And call the second part as your HTML page's head. Every web page that you can see on the net are composed of these two parts. The tags that you have learned in the previous chapter are part of your HTML's body.

As you can see on the example, the head and body tag are nested inside the html tag. The head goes in first, while the body is the last one to appear. The order of the two is essential to your web page.

When coding in HTML, you should always place or nest all the tags or elements that your visitors will see on your HTML's body tag. On the other hand, any script or JavaScript code and styling line or CSS line that your visitors will not see must go into the head tag.

Scripts and styling lines must be read first by your browser. Even before the browser displays all the elements in your body tag, it must be already stylized and the scripts should be ready. And that is why the head tag goes first before the body.

If you place the styling lines on the end of the page, the browser may behave differently. For example, if the styling lines are placed at the end, the browser will display the elements on the screen first, and then once it reads the styling lines, the appearance of the page will change. On the other hand, if a button on your page gets clicked before the scripts for it was loaded because the scripts are placed on the end of the document, the browser will return an error.

Browsers and Checking the Source Code

Fortunately, if you forget to place the html, head, and body tags, modern browsers will automatically generate them for you. For example, try opening the HTML file that you created without the three tags with Google Chrome.

Once you open your file, press the F12 key to activate the developer console. As you can see, the html, head, and body tags were already generated for you in order to display your HTML file properly.

By the way, checking source codes is an important method that you should always use if you want to learn or imitate a website's HTML code. You can easily do it by using the developer console on Chrome or by using the context menu on other browsers and clicking on the View Page Source or View Source option.

Document Type Declaration

HTML has undergone multiple versions. As of now, the latest version is HTML5. With each version, some tags are introduced while some are deprecated. And some versions come with specifications that make them behave differently from each other. Because of that, HTML documents must include a document type declaration to make sure that your markup will be displayed just the way you wanted them to appear on your visitors' screens.

However, you do not need to worry about this a lot since it will certainly stick with HTML5, which will not be discussed in full in this book. In HTML5, document type declaration is useless, but is required. To satisfy this, all you need to do is place this on the beginning of your HTML files:

<!DOCTYPE html>

With all of those laid out, you can now create proper HTML documents. In the following chapters, the book will focus on providing you the tags that you will use the most while web developing.

Chapter 4: More HTML Tags

Now, it is time to make your HTML file to appear like a typical web page on the internet. And you can do that by learning the tags and attributes that are used in websites you stumble upon while you surf the web.

The Title Tag

First of all, you should give your web page a title. You can do that by using the <title> tag. The title of the page can be seen on the title bar and tab on your browser. If you bookmark your page, it will become the name of the bookmark. Also, it will appear on your taskbar if the page is active.

When using the title tag, place it inside the head tag. Below is an example:

```
<head>
	<title>This Is My New Web Page</title>
</head>
```

The Header Tags

If you want to organize the hierarchy of your titles and text on your web page's article, then you can take advantage of the header tags. If you place a line of text inside header tags, its formatting will change. Its font size will become bigger and its font weight (thickness) will become heavier. For example:

```
<h1> This Is the Title of This Article</h1>
<p>This is the introductory paragraph. This is another sentence. And
this is the last sentence.</p>
```

If you try this example, this is what you will get:

This Is the Title of This Article

This is the introductory paragraph. This is another sentence. And this is the last sentence.

There are six levels of heading tags and they are: <h1>,<h2>,<h3>,<h4>,<h5>, and <h6>. Each level has different formatting. And as the level gets higher, the lesser formatting will be applied.

The Image Tag

First, start with pictures. You can insert pictures in your web page by using the <img> tag. By the way, the <img> tag is one of HTML tags that do not need closing tags, which are called null or empty tags. And for you to see how it works, check the example below:

```
<img
src=”http://upload.wikimedia.org/wikipedia/commons/thumb/8/80
/Wikipedia-logo-v2.svg/150px-Wikipedia-logo-v2.svg.png” >
```

If you try that code and opened your HTML file, the Wikipedia logo will appear. As you can see, the <img> tag did not need a closing tag to work. As long as you place a valid value on its src (source) attribute, then an image will appear on your page. In case an image file is not present on the URL you placed on the source attribute, then a broken image picture will appear instead.

Image Format Tips

By the way, the <img> tag can display pictures with the following file types: PNG, JPEG or JPG, and GIF. Each image type has characteristics that you can take advantage of. If you are going to post photographs, it is best to convert them to JPG file format. The JPG offers decent file compression that can reduce the size of your photographs without losing too much quality.

If you need lossless quality or if you want to display a photo or image as is, then you should use PNG. The biggest drawback on PNG is that old browsers cannot read PNG images. But that is almost a thing of a past since only handful people use old versions of browsers.

On the other hand, if you want animated images on your site, then use GIFs. However, take note that the quality of GIF is not that high. The number of colors it can display is few unlike PNG and JPG. But because of that, its size is comparatively smaller than the two formats, which is why some web developers convert their sites' logos as GIF to conserve space and reduce loading time.

The Ordered and Unordered List

Surely, you will place lists on your web pages sooner or later. In HTML, you can create two types of lists: ordered and unordered. Ordered lists generate alphanumeric characters to denote sequence on your list while unordered lists generate symbols that only change depending on the list level.

To create ordered lists, use the <ol> and <li> tag. The <ol> tag defines that the list will be an ordered one, and the <li> or list item tag defines that its content is considered a list item on the list. Below is an example:

```
<h1>Animals</h1>
<ol>
	<li>dog</li>
	<li>cat</li>
	<li>mouse</li>
</ol>
```

This will be the result of that example:

Animals

1. dog
2. cat
3. mouse

On the other hand, if you want an unordered list, you will need to use the <ul> tag. Like the <ol> tag, you will still need to use the <li> tag to denote the list items. Below is an example:

```
<h1>Verbs</h1>
<ul>
	<li>walk</li>
	<li>jog</li>
	<li>run</li>
</ul>
```

This will be the result of that example:

Verbs

- walk
- jog
- run

Instead of numbers, the list used bullets instead. If ever you use the <li> tag without <ol> or <ul>, browsers will usually create them as unordered lists.

Nesting Lists

You can nest lists in HTML to display child lists. If you do that, the browser will accommodate it and apply the necessary tabs for the child list items. If you nest unordered lists, the bullets will be changed to fit the child list items. Below is an example:

```
<h1>Daily Schedule</h1>
<ul>
	<li>Morning</li>

	<ul>
		<li>Jog</li>
		<li>Shower</li>
		<li>Breakfast</li>
	</ul>
	<li>Afternoon</li>
	<ul>
		<li>Lunch</li>
		<li>Watch TV</li>
```

```
    </ul>
    <li>Evening</li>
    <ul>
        <li>Dinner</li>
        <li>Sleep</li>
    </ul>
</ul>
```

This will be the result of that example:

Daily Schedule

- Morning
    - Jog
    - Shower
    - Breakfast
- Afternoon
    - Lunch
    - Watch TV
- Evening
    - Dinner
    - Sleep

And with that, you should be ready to create a decent website of your own. But for now, practice using those tags. And experiment with them.

Conclusion

Thank you again for purchasing this book!

I hope this book was able to help you to become knowledgeable when it comes to HTML development. With the fundamentals you have learned, you can easily explore the vast and enjoyable world of web development. And that is no exaggeration.

The next step is to learn more tags and check out websites' sources. Also, look for HTML development tips. Then learn more about HTML5 and schema markup. Those things will help you create richer web sites that are semantically optimized.

On the other hand, if you want to make your website to look cool, then you can jump straight to leaning CSS or Cascading Style Sheets. Cascading Style Sheets will allow you to define the appearance of all or each element in your web page. You can change font size, weight, color, and family of all the text on your page in a whim. You can even create simple animations that can make your website look modern and fancy.

If you want your website to be interactive, then you can start learning client side scripting with JavaScript or Jscript too. Scripts will provide your web pages with functions that can make it more alive. An example of a script function is when you press a button on your page, a small window will popup.

Once you master all of that, then it will be the best time for you to start learning server side scripting such as PHP or ASP. With server side scripting, you can almost perform everything on websites. You can take information from forms and save them to your database. Heck, you can even create dynamic web pages. Or even add chat functions on your website.

Finally, if you enjoyed this book, please take the time to share your thoughts and post a review on Amazon. We do our best to reach out to readers and provide the best value we can. Your positive review will help us achieve that. It'd be greatly appreciated!

Thank you and good luck!

Check Out My Other Books

Below you'll find some of my other popular books that are popular on Amazon and Kindle as well. Simply click on the links below to check them out. Alternatively, you can visit my author page on Amazon to see other work done by me.

C Programming Success in a Day

Android Programming in a Day

C Programming Professional Made Easy

C ++ Programming Success in a Day

Python Programming in a Day

PHP Programming Professional Made Easy

JavaScript Programming Made Easy

CSS Programming Professional Made Easy

Windows 8 Tips for Beginners

If the links do not work, for whatever reason, you can simply search for these titles on the Amazon website to find them.

www.ingramcontent.com/pod-product-compliance
Lightning Source LLC
Chambersburg PA
CBHW060931050326
40689CB00013B/3042
* 9 7 8 1 5 1 8 6 4 5 5 9 4 *